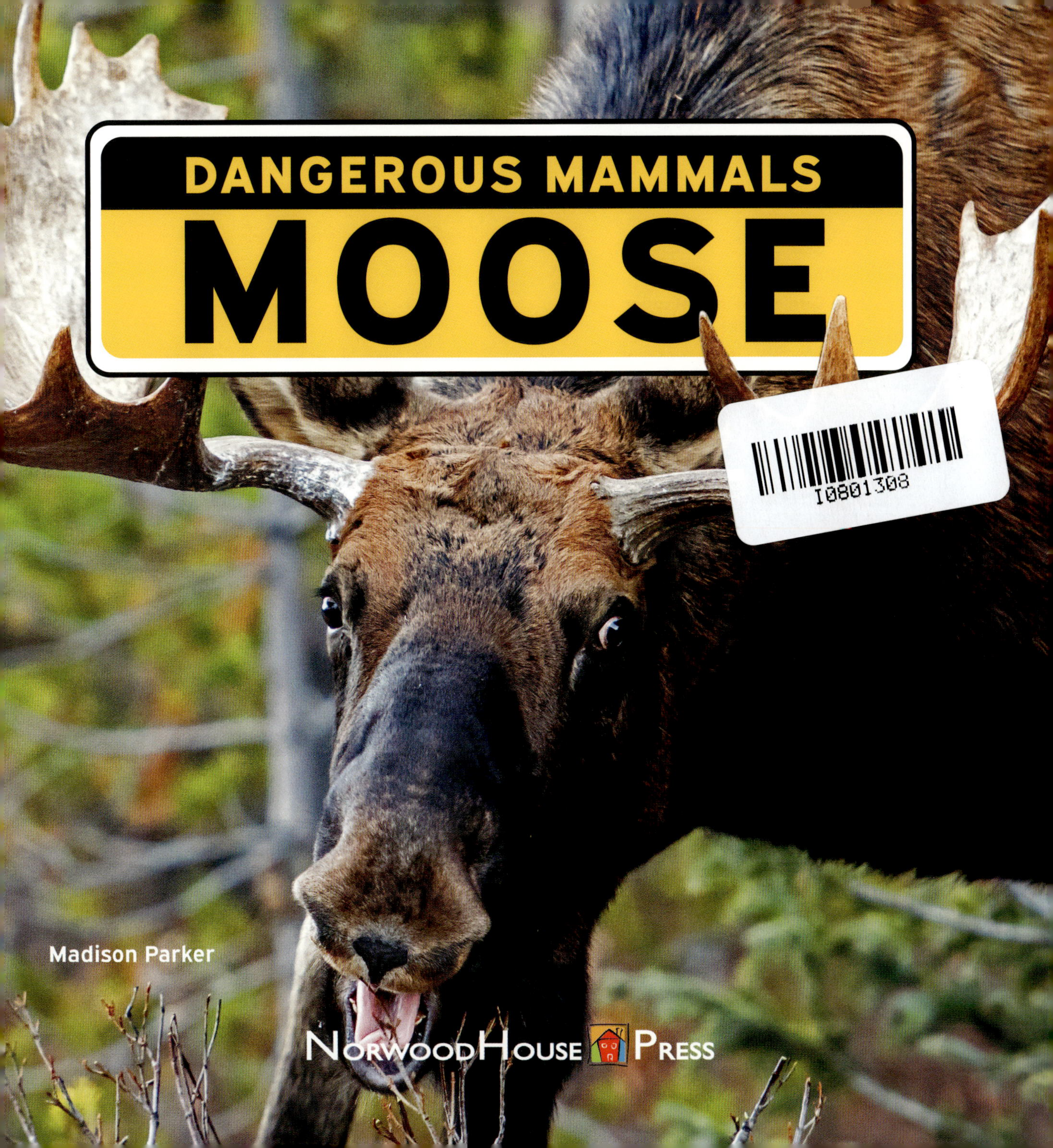

DANGEROUS MAMMALS

MOOSE

Madison Parker

NorwoodHouse Press

Library of Congress Cataloging-in-Publication Data:

Names: Parker, Madison.
Title: Moose / Madison Parker.
Description: Buffalo, NY : Norwood House Press, 2025. | Series: Dangerous mammals | Includes glossary and index.
Identifiers: ISBN 9781684502622 (pbk.) | ISBN 9781684502639 (library bound) | ISBN 9781684502646 (ebook)
Subjects: LCSH: Moose--Juvenile literature.
Classification: LCC QL737.U55 P375 2025 | DDC 599.65'7--dc23

Published in 2025 by
Norwood House Press
2544 Clinton Street
Buffalo, NY 14224

Designer: Ocean Books
Editor: Kim Thompson

Photo credits: Cover, p. 1 Ghost Bear/Shutterstock.com; p. 5 Harry Collins Photography/Shutterstock.com; p. 6 mark stephens photography/Shutterstock.com; p. 7 Michael Liggett/Shutterstock.com; p. 9 Renee Foskett/Shutterstock.com; p. 10 Tom Tietz/Shutterstock.com; p. 11 Thomas Konopasek/Shutterstock.com; p. 12 pathan daraksha khan/Shutterstock.com; p. 13 Paul Tessier; p. 15 irakite/Shutterstock.com; p. 16 Mark Byer/Shutterstock.com; p. 17 Szczepan Klejbuk/Shutterstock.com; p. 19 Elle777/Shutterstock.com; p. 21 ImPoto/Shutterstock.com

Printed in the United States of America

CPSIA compliance information: Batch #CW25NHP: For further information contact Norwood House Press at 1-800-237-9932.

TABLE OF CONTENTS

MEET THE MOOSE

A moose is a large **mammal** with long legs, a huge head, and a hump on its back. A skin flap on its neck is called a bell. Male moose grow **antlers**.

TYPES OF MOOSE

The Eastern moose is dark brown. It lives in the forests of Maine and Canada. It can be dangerous when it feels **threatened**, especially during **mating** season.

Western moose are light brown. They live in Alaska and in the Rocky Mountains. If they are surprised while they are eating, they can get **aggressive**.

Alaskan moose are the largest. They live in Alaska and western Canada. If they feel trapped or if they are protecting babies, they can be dangerous.

The small Shiras moose has lighter fur on its legs and face. It lives in mountains in the western United States. If it feels scared, it can **charge**.

European moose live in Scandinavia and Eastern Europe. They can be a danger to drivers because they often cross roads.

The Siberian moose roams the forests of northern Asia. It has thick, dark fur. It can be aggressive during mating season.

The large Eastern European moose lives in Poland and the Baltic states. It is **territorial** and can be dangerous during mating season.

FAVORITE FOODS

Moose eat leaves from trees and shrubs. They also munch on the bark of young trees. Their long legs help them reach high branches.

In summer, moose eat water plants. They wade into lakes and ponds to get them. These plants are soft and easy for moose to **digest**.

In winter, moose eat pine cones and pine needles. They dig through the snow to find moss.

STAYING SAFE AROUND MOOSE

Moose are big and fast. If you see one, stay far away. Always watch from a distance. If a moose charges, run and hide behind a tree.

Moose can be aggressive if they feel threatened. Never try to touch a moose or its babies.

If you are in moose territory, keep dogs on a leash. Moose get upset if a dog annoys them. Drive slowly and watch for moose on the road.

GLOSSARY

aggressive (uh-GRES-iv): threatening; ready to attack

antlers (ANT-lurz): large, branching, bony structures on the heads of deer, moose, or elk

charge (chahrj): to attack in a rush

digest (dye-JEST): to break down food in the stomach and intestines so it can be used by the body

mammal (MAM-uhl): an animal that is warm-blooded, that has hair or fur, that usually gives birth to live babies, and that produces milk to feed its babies

mating (MAY-ting): joining together to produce babies

territorial (ter-i-TOR-ee-uhl): inclined to occupy and defend an area of land, often land that contains an animal's nest, den, or home

threatened (THRE-tuhnd): in danger of being harmed

THINKING QUESTIONS

1. Why are moose mammals?
2. What kinds of food do moose like to eat?
3. What should you do if you see a moose?
4. How are Eastern moose and Siberian moose alike and different?
5. Where do moose live?

INDEX

ABOUT THE AUTHOR

Madison Parker spent her childhood in the city of Chicago, Illinois. A farm girl at heart, today she lives in Wisconsin with her husband and four children on a small farm with cows, goats, chickens, and two miniature horses named Harley and David. Her favorite dessert is vanilla frozen custard with rainbow sprinkles, even in the winter.